The Adventures of Lightning the Cat

Short Stories Collection 1
Lightning's Job, The Battle of the Tomato,
and Disarmament

By Teresa Garcia

THG StarDragon Publishing

via Createspace

Paperback Edition

Copyright 2012

ISBN-13: 978-1480296824

About the Adventures of Lightning the Cat

Lightning's adventures is a series of short short stories centered around Lightning, an actual caregiver kitty, his family, and his friends. A lover of tomatoes and mischief, he often has little mini adventures, and sometimes is not entirely sure of the normality of his family. Not all of his adventures have made it to the page yet, so be sure to check in on him often. Perhaps he might even write out a few of his adventures himself.

Dedication

This story is for my daughter Athena, and her friends. Lightning the Cat is real, as are many of his friends. His adventures too, are real (unless he's writing one and making himself look even better, then I can't guarantee it). My thanks to Joseph Campbell, author of "Loony Coon," for showing me through his books that it is perfectly possible to write true stories of animals and have them be appreciated. My thanks also to my departed Father, Ben Garcia, for having given me his copy of "Loony Coon" when I was small. This is a paperback version of the longer Smashwords edition, as per the request of Athena and her friends. The first edition was much shorter, as there was a word limit on the contest it had been submitted for, and it still available on Lulu.

Contents

The Adventures of Lightning the Cat

Lightning's Job

Lightning's Job

A sneeze rent the air, accompanied by a loud creak and even louder thud. Opening his golden eyes to slits, the sight that greeted him was his mother's mother on her back, legs and black socked feet dangling over the edge of the upturned desk chair. The wheels still spun as she rolled out and stood shakily, grabbing a tissue and blowing her nose before turning her chair back right side up.

Just another day in early winter.

Lightning closed his eyes again, snuggling down into the HP printer that he liked to nap on, his white and orange fur contrasting with the black plastic. Clicking and tapping resumed at a swift pace, and opening his eyes once more, he saw the black clothed and pale skinned mistress of the house busy with her assignments.

Too busy. She had begun to forget to feed herself as of late, though the human children that also dwelled here, his mother and uncle, she never forgot to feed. Ever. Lightning sneezed, a deliberate comment on her homework, and closed his eyes again, posing. The computer sounds ceased for a moment.

"What?" Mother's voice, quiet from disuse and long habit,

floated to him.

He shifted imperiously.

"Oh... alright."

The creaking of the chair and the sliding of the keyboard shelf being pushed back below her desk warned him, before the slender hand arrived, that the human had misunderstood, still brain fried no doubt from the pace of her assignments lately. He held back a purr as the cool hand ran over his fur and her voice broke out into sweet nonsense syllables. Lightning rolled over, presenting his white belly for stroking.

He mewled imperiously and pinned her with his hopeful gaze, then blinked and wiggled.

"Who's the cutest kitty in the world? Who's such a good study buddy? Lightning is, that's who. Yes you are. I bet you'd like a treat. How's a snack sound?"

He was scooped off of his warm printer perch and against the ribbed black sweater, cradled in slim arms that carried him to the kitchen before setting him down. Soon enough, the smell of chicken bits filled the air as they landed in his bowl, and a fresh bowl of water was also presented itself in short order.

Lightning turned his nose up, though his stomach growled loudly in protest, and stalked over to the white refrigerator. He rose up on his hind legs and reached for the handle with his forelegs, grumbling loudly at only having paws instead of hands with opposable thumbs like his mother and Mother had. It was only then that Mother's stomach replied to his growl.

"Oh... I hadn't realized how much time had passed already. Thank you for keeping track."

Mother opened the door and began rummaging for something to fix herself, as he stalked back to his own food and began to eat, purring loudly and closing his eyes to press out a wide kitty smile. By the time he had finished and began to clean his face, Mother had made a stout tuna sandwich, packed with far too many vegetables for his taste.

The tomato hanging out the side did look pretty tempting though, and so he curled his tail and mewed as prettily as he could, lifting a paw and gesturing at it.

"Noo... this is my tomato. You stole the last one when Daughter forgot to close the fridge door after her snack yesterday..."

Lightning put his paw down and pouted, lowering his ears as pitifully as he could.

"Oh... alright... just a little..." She pulled part of her tomato out, setting it in his dish and patting his head. "You're a spoiled kitty."

He mrowed. He earned every bit of that, with all the hard

work he had in making sure everyone's needs were met. Care kitties were busy kitties, even when their person was off at school.

Mother walked back to the desk in her bedroom, after refilling her coffee, and took her food along. Lightning perked his ears up, finished his chicken, then delicately picked up what was left of his tomato and hauled it along. The sounds of the keyboard hadn't started just yet, but he was determined that she eat before the others came home.

As expected, she had her nose in the textbook, sandwich halfway to her mouth. Putting his tomato down on the brown carpet, he lashed his tail, before rearing up to try seeing what the squiggly lines were this time.

He thought it was the "History" book. Who knew though, she always went on about International Somethings, and especially some societies that lived way over the Pacific. He knew where Japan was though. She pointed countries out on maps often to Son and Daughter, whether they cared or not.

Lightning growled loudly and hissed, Mother started and took a bite of her sandwich. He returned to his tomato and gobbled it, growling again whenever she paused in her eating too long. This thing called a "Degree" really bugged him.

"I hope it comes with a big fat fish when she finally earns it..."

Mother finally finished her lunch. He went to the bathroom and used his litterbox, then went to the door, meowing until Mother got up to let him out for his rounds.

He considered these gravely important. Though there were other cats, he patrolled for mice that would try to get into the buildings of the complex. He visited some of the elderly people too. Lightning was even known, once in a while, to let some of the chubby toddling youngsters give him a stroke or two when they passed by with their parents. Once he made sure that all was in order, and that his favorites were in decent moods, he would bask in the sun. His favorite spot was the walk in front of their building, where he could greet the other families in the apartments, and watch for Daughter.

Lightning stretched out full and napped. He moved when Mother came down to start a cartful of laundry, and escorted her there. Every once in a while she was known to fall, due to the way the cold sometimes made her joints lock and catch. Today she moved without a cane, for which he was glad.

As usual, he tried to slip into the laundry room when she got to that building. As usual, she nudged him out and reminded him he needed to stay out. So he sprawled in front of the door and continued his guard duty. If she fell, he would go get someone to follow him and bring help. It was, after all, what a care kitty was supposed to do. Happily, she did not fall or get stuck though, and he escorted her back before resuming his watch.

At last, after long hours of waiting, school was out. He could hear the bell on the school just blocks away announcing the release of the children. Cats and dogs all over the town listened keenly for this, as it announced the return of their children.

Lightning stood. He stretched. He yawned. Then he padded his way for the gate of the apartment complex to meet his Person. As it was winter he didn't have to walk and watch for the snakes that sometimes came to town, but he still liked to go greet her now and then. Especially if she'd been having trouble at school lately, or when there had been the weird stomach problems that kept Mother up worrying over.

Teresa Garcia

The Adventures of Lightning the Cat

The Battle of the Tomato

The Battle of the Tomato

Once again, his mother figure, Daughter, and uncle figure, Son, were at school. Once again, Mother, the mistress of the house, was ensconced at her desk working frantically. Lightning, however, neither was ensconced at a desk, nor working. Instead, he was firmly and comfortably ensconced in the porch chair, snuggled into the black and blue flowered cushion, listening to the world go by.

It was a good day to be a cat. The sky was a vivid blue that contrasted prettily against the green of the surrounding pine needles. The breeze blew softly, bathing him with a warm stream, ruffling his fur only lightly. His whiskers tingled and flicked in pleasure, matched by his keen ears as they picked up birdsong.

Nearby birdsong.

Lightning's gold eyes opened at the butter soft padding of paws coming up the stairwell. Another pair of gold eyes peeked over the topmost bit, framed in fluffy black, slightly bedraggled, black and white fur. This was followed in short order they the rest of the body, and soon enough, Squeakers, the tailless cat that was one of his neighbors, slinked over and sat before him.

She blinked at him slowly. "Nice day for a nap."

Lightning looked at her, then licked his white right fore-paw lightly, making sure to move in just the right way to showcase his orange and white markings for her. "It is. Would be a good day to chase birds too."

"They're up too high in the pines, and don't stay long enough in the lower trees."

Lightning yawned and resigned himself to waiting a few more days to try sneaking up on one of the raucous ravens that inhabited the neighborhood. "I've still not forgiven when one tried to take off with some of Mother's hair," he said, matter-of-factly.

"I think she taught them well enough when she talked back to them and mocked them in their own language. They don't even poop on her car anymore." Squeaker laid down and rolled over, looking up at him lazily.

"Still," he looked down at her with lazy interest, his tail twitching only slightly, "They knew better than to mess with Mother."

"It's what they do."

The cats rested companionably on the breezeway, listening to the frantic tapping coming from inside the apartment. After a while, the sounds ceased, and there was the creak of a chair and the floor as Mother stood up. Soon enough, the sound of the refrigerator door opening, and of a plate being set out, rang through the air.

"Lunch. BRB." Lightning moaned, getting up and stretching, before jaunting in to see what he could snag.

"BRB?" Squeakers mused to herself as she waited. "Oh, you mean 'be right back.' You know I hate text speak. I can't spell." She grumbled, knowing it would do no good as his mistress/mother tended to speak it fluently.

Inside, Lightning discovered Mother busily crafting herself a BLT sandwich. The bacon was just starting to sizzle, the enticing aroma beginning to waft through the apartment. He rose up on his hind legs and rested his forepaws on the deceptively empty blue jeans, long used to aiming dead center to prevent a fall. Lightning meowed as prettily as he could, putting on his best smile and eye sparkle.

"MY bacon, kitty. That works on little one but not me."

She paused in slicing the juicy tomato, which he eyed with keen interest, to get down a can of his wet cat food. A pop and metallic peeling sound grated his ears, his nose getting deliciously coated in the oily scent of fish, and he eagerly took the opportunity to jump up on the counter while Mother was busy doling out his lunch.

By the time she turned around to get him down, he was already chomping and licking merrily on the tomato she'd barely gotten even one slice from.

"CAT!"

Lightning tried to take it with him, when he jumped down and scampered off, but it was too heavy. SPLAT! Juicy red tomato thudded to the floor like a handful of Gack, or so it sounded to him. There was a loud groan as Mother set to salvaging what she could. He peeked around the corner, watching for his opportunity.

When she took the tomato bulk to the sink to wash it off, he struck. Streaking in, tail like a banner, he then slid between her legs and stopped where the juice hadn't been mopped up.

"Fine, go for it you little nutter..." Mother grumbled, patting down the salvaged remains before turning to flip her bacon. "Less for me to clean up if you drink up the pulp..."

"Yes..." Lightning purred, doing just that as Squeakers padded into the apartment through the open door.

"Oh, hello Squeakers. Loud is it?"

Squeakers nodded her head sagely.

"Sorry about that. You know how it is. Lightning and his tomato obsession."

Squeakers nodded again, sitting as prettily as she could, and meowed, eying Lightning's dish.

"You may as well. He's got a mess he's tending to."

Squeakers padded eagerly over to the cat dish, gingerly beginning to eat. Once she had nibbled her fill, she resumed watching her friend. Lightning was busily licking the dregs off the floor, hard enough she was certain tile bits were going to start sticking in his tongue.

Mother finished slicing up tomato for her sandwich, and layered her toppings. Finally, she set the bacon to drain, bagged the remaining tomato, and placed it in the fridge. Lightning eyed the door, his whiskers drooping. Squeakers shook her head, mewed a thanks to the human, and padded back outside, deciding that her visit was over.

"I'll see you later tomato-boy, Ruby will need escorting soon."

"Later, Squeakers."

Mother finished putting together her, now huge, sandwich, and carried the blue plate back off to her room. The rustling of paper from there told him that though she was eating, she was looking up something for some paper she was researching for.

"At least she's remembering to eat... Now, let's see..."

Lightning hemmed and hawed in front of the refrigerator a few moments, devising his plan of attack. Hanging on the door handle had no effect, nor did his commanding mrows. At last, frustrated, he pushed at where the seal was.

His eyes sprang wide when the white box popped open, and the cool air and scent of various foods, some less appetizing than others, flowed out. Quickly, he peered in.

No tomato. Yet, he could smell it, ripe and sweet, water packed and beckoning. Frantically he began to paw at drawers, till at last he managed to get one open. To his delight, there lay several tomatoes, each quietly singing his name.

"What on earth is all that racket cat?"

"Uh oh..."

He latched his teeth into the one that had already been gotten into, able now to lift it due to how much had been cut away, and galloped out of the apartment and down the steps, leaving the fridge wide open.

"Lighting!"

The Adventures of Lightning the Cat

Disarmament

Disarmament

It was a fine day to be a cat. The sky was the high blue of summer, and Mt Shasta still had a bit of snow, melting in the sun's heat, visibly staining brown at the edges. The birds were out, and a slight breeze ghosted around the apartment complex to dash over the lawn and through the trees. Yet, despite the blue, there were still clouds, and the mugginess and temperament of the breeze spoke of oncoming storms.

It was also a laundry day.

Bang! Bang! Bang!

Ah, there it was, the sound of the black wire cart being negotiated down the stairs, and two voices accompanied it, talking about whatever it was that humans talked about. Lightning lazily looked toward the source from his spot on the grass, alone since his friends were all off lounging elsewhere.

"Careful mom. You fall."

The light voice of the boy child, his "uncle" sounded worried. Mother had probably lost her balance a bit on the stairs again, trying to manage the load. The voices and banging soon made their way to the foot of the stairs, and the banging stopped.

"Thank you little one. Such a helper. We don't need mommy breaking her hip, do we?"

"No. I help you!"

With that, the little boy, clad only in shorts and socks, tore off for the laundry room. Lightning stretched and yawned, exposing needle sharp hunter's teeth. Mother passed by with her cart of clothes and blankets, two loads worth, then he padded after her, tail high and gold eyes gleaming. As usual, there was a hitch in her step, but this time it seemed that she was having to favor her good side more often than her left side.

"Mrow?"

Mother stopped, then bent down carefully to pet him, grimacing a bit. He wondered if she'd taken her pills, or if she was being stubborn again. By the faces she always made when swallowing them, he knew she didn't like them, despite how much they helped if she took them soon enough.

"Good kitty." Her hand stroked his orange and white fur briefly, and he threaded around her ankles soothingly. She nodded. "I'll take them again when I get back upstairs. No idea why I hurt so bad today. Maybe a storm's comin'."

He twitched his tail in acknowledgment, and she continued on. Ahead, the chubby boy with the unruly brownish hair and bright brown eyes held the blue door open with all the pomp he could muster.

"Mommies first!" He piped, beaming proudly. "Oh, there's

Lightning. Good kitty. He will guard us while we deliver the load."

"Um... Ok... Thank you, Son."

She went in, and then the boy delivered a speech, which he apparently felt of great import. Lightning understood none of it. He pretended though, nodding his head at Son and sitting pertly. He thought that it might be something about those robot Transformers that he liked so much that he filled the house with, but he wasn't sure. The boy was speaking clearer all the time, after all the work at home and the special school program, but there was still much that not even Mother or Daughter ever understood.

He didn't care. Even though the boy got rough sometimes, and often jibbered confusingly, he was still family. The speech ended, and Lightning nodded again, standing up, then meowed importantly. The door closed, Mother already busily loading the washers. Once the door was closed, he relocated slightly, then stretched back out on the concrete walk.

Mr A, the complex maintenance man, walked by and opened the door to the maintenance side of that building. He paused and looked at the orange and white ball of sleek fur and hunter's muscle.

"We guarding today, or taking a break from patrol?"

Lightning blinked his gold eyes slowly, then looked toward

the laundry room door, then bad at Mr A before meowing. Son was getting worked up, and they could make out something like "Hurry Mom. Incoming."

"Ah, carry on then. Good kitty. If you find any mice give 'em what for."

Mr A then went in and began to choose his tools for his repair project. There was always something to work on at Water Street. Lightning closed his eyes and purred contentedly. The cement he sprawled on was just right, there was shade, and he could smell the flowers.

After a bit, Mother and Son came out, sans the now empty laundry cart. They only went a few steps down the walk before Lightning observed the little boy's arm gut check his mother.

"Wait Mom! It trap."

"Trap?" Mother looked in the direction the boy pointed, and he could see her momentary confusion. Lightning looked as well, perhaps his superior cat-vision could see something that human eyes behind thick glasses didn't.

No such luck. All he saw was grass, cement sidewalk, flowers, parked cars, and the buildings. No traps whatsoever. He got up and stretched.

"Magic traps. They must have set them while we inside. Wait for Lightning!"

He walked past the two calmly. Whether the boy was just playing, or whether he thought it was real, it was all the same to Lightning. This was just another part of his Very Important Job.

"Lightning will save us. He knows what to do, just you watch Mom. He will disarm them."

He twitched his tail. "That's right. Because that's my job, taking care of all of you." It didn't matter to him that they probably didn't understand what he said.

When he was perhaps five feet ahead, he stopped and pawed at the ground, as if digging up something, even though digging in cement was impossible. He made the biggest show he could, and then made it bigger by chasing circles for a bit before continuing on to repeat the process. Each time, Lightning was careful to puff himself up even bigger.

"You're right, he *does* know just what to do. Such a smart cat."

He could tell Mother knew it was just for show that he was playing along. The boy was making an effort to interact though, so he would reward him this way. Lightning winked at her, then strutted the rest of the way to the stairs while his humans followed.

"Lightning is so cool, Mom. He takes good care of us."

"Yes, he's a very special kitty." Mother bent down to pet him, and he rubbed into her hand and against the railing, then padded up to watch from the top.

"Can we give him some fish? He was really brave."

"Alright. I think he earned a treat."

They came up the stairs and opened the door, the little boy burbling and following his mother all the way to the kitchen. Lightning followed too. There would be just enough time to eat his treat before going to meet Daughter on her way back. And then he would love all over her while she petted him, no doubt getting covered with his hair, and he could listen to her tell him about her adventures.

About the Author

Teresa Garcia is a 30-something mother of two children with special needs (one is autistic, the other has chronic depression and anxiety issues at far too young an age), raising them "alone" in the small mountain town of McCloud, CA. Just because she is on her own though, does not mean that she is "alone." Many thanks are due to the McCloud Community Resource Center, to her brother and his family, and her mother, for all their help.

When not drowning in university coursework for her International Relations degree, and chained to the computer, she loves to text role play with her long distance mate Vadise, write stories, hike, paint, meditate, and play games or read with her kids. She also writes quests for, and helps to maintain, the online browser-based RPG Dragon Hearts.

She was raised in another mountain community, which she visits as often as she can spare time and gas, though not nearly often enough for her wishes. Her parents always encouraged her writing and artistic talents. In 2005, she decided to pick up the dream of writing and publishing a novel once more, having shelved that (and the "Shadow Chronicles" manuscript) in her early college years due to the time constraints of motherhood at the time. In 2006 she released to the public her first novel in the

"Dragon Shaman" series, "Taming the Blowing Wind," and has since published a second book in the series and a poetry book.

Currently Teresa has several manuscripts to work on, such as her "Dragon Shaman" series of novels and her current favorite serialized story, "Selkies' Skins."

More about her works can be found at

https://www.smashwords.com/profile/view/Amehana

and http://www.thgstardragon.com.

She also can be found on twitter at

https://twitter.com/#!/AmehanaArashi,

or on the THG StarDragon Publishing Facebook page.

Her personal blog is located at http//rainstardragon.livejournal.com

She also happily accepts snail mail:

THG StarDragon Publishing

Attn: Teresa Garcia

PO Box 249

McCloud, CA 96057

USA

or email:

ladyrainstardragon@hotmail.com

Please fill out the subject line, to prevent it from being thought to be spam.

Forthcoming Works

Dragon Shaman

Book Three: The Forge and Well

Marie and Marcella O'Drake, two of the descendants of an ancient Irish Priestess, are chosen from their family to become the caretakers of Brigid's Forge and Well. Marie, young modern woman that she is, can not accept, nor can she accept her families supposed insanity. However, Fate itself can not be denied, no matter how one runs from it, and it will follow.

Selkies' Skins

What happens if a Selkie never gets her skin back? Will Etain come home, and will Kirsty earn a sealskin and survive? A journey begins.

Explore the Kickstarter and be part of the creative process: http://kck.st/ToLpqL

Available Works

Dragon Shaman

Book One: Taming the Blowing Wind

Long ago, an Irish Priestess was defiled, and the dragon that had become her protector laid a terrible curse upon the children of the man responsible. His curse, laid in anger, had severe repercussions for himself, and the children of the woman he loved. In the present, one of the children of the interloper's seed must follow the spirit of her own love to break the curse on her family. BlowingWind meets Take Ryu, and old family patterns begin to be woven again.

Book Two: The Smoky Mirror

Continuing her adventures, BlowingWind traverses both worlds and time itself to regain the Smoky Mirror. A Kitsune and a pair of Tengu complicate matters for her and Ryu, engaged in their own jobs. In the process, BlowingWind learns a bit more about her family, and why it is as it is. Will she remember what is important when and if she returns to the normal world, or will the world of spirits claim her forever?

Call of the Kami

A poetry book exploring spirituality, dragon lore, and nature, where East and West intertwine.

Also look for other works by Teresa Garcia (or Teresa Huddleston-Garcia) at Amazon, Lulu, and Smashwords.

Don't forget to look for other authors with THG StarDragon Publishing!

Chapter 1: Morning Plans

Excerpt from Dragon Shaman Book Two

Starlight streamed through the open window to spill across the tossed sheets and pale face that he watched, lending the narrow visage its silver luminescence. Her short auburn hair was dark in the night, a far cry from the daytime highlights of red, like a swirl of fertile earth beneath the rich loam outside of the cabin. A stray moonbeam refracted off of his dark eyes, shining like foxfire as he ran a hand through his midnight hair and guarded her restless dreams.

"You're supposed to let me into them BlowingWind."

She frowned in her sleep, rolling over to her side and away from him, counting on his honor to restrain him on the other side of the sword lurking between them. The luminescent oval of his own pale face smiled beneath the night dark spikes of contained energy where it rested on his hand, his body perilously close to the keen blade.

"I suppose that I could leave you in Tokyo safely

while I set up our new home in Hokkaido. The time alone will be good for you, and you can learn for yourself how entwined you are with me. I will still be easily available if you need me though."

The growls of her dreams died away slowly as she conquered whatever minor demon she had been facing. The mask of her anger fell away again, revealing the child hiding within the woman whose loneliness had called him to her side only a few short weeks ago, or perhaps it was months now with the way time flowed so strangely between his world and hers.

"Besides, even though we have reunited the four major parts of your spirit, you still feel incomplete. If I let you be for a month, perhaps you will be able to feel some sense of where the dust and shards of your soul-jewel have scattered to, my precious tama."

BlowingWind retreated beneath the covers, pulling them over her head as if even in her dreams his constant watch was annoying. Incoherent mumbles came from underneath the blankets, then faded to nothing.

"What is it you don't want me to know Little One?"

Silence was his only answer from the sleeping woman, and the night danced silently on as he brooded over his prized gem. When night had finally left and the sun intruded into the rustic bedroom with her spears of light, BlowingWind rolled over again. Restless legs stretched out from the ball she had curled into, bringing the blankets down and exposing her once more to his penetrating stare. The itch on her skin that his gaze produced caused blinking and bleary eyes to search for the irritant.

"Ah! You didn't stare at me all night, did you Ryu?"

"I prefer to think of it as 'brooding.' It's a dragon thing."